The IT Infrastructure Library

# An Introductory Overview of I

Version 1.0

| | | |
|---|---|---|
| Written by: | Alis | |
| | Ash | |
| | Coli. | ıtEMS Ltd |
| | Ivor Macfarlane | IBM |
| | John Windebank | Sun |
| | Stuart Rance | IIP |
| Edited by: | Alison Cartlidge | Xansa - Steria |
| | Mark Lillycrop | itSMF UK |
| Published by: | The UK Chapter of the itSMF | |

With thanks to all those who took part in the review process.

# About this guide

ITIL (IT Infrastructure Library) provides a framework of Best Practice guidance for IT Service Management and since its creation, ITIL has grown to become the most widely accepted approach to IT Service Management in the world.

This pocket guide has been designed as an introductory overview for anyone who has an interest in or a need to understand more about the objectives, content and coverage of ITIL. Whilst this guide provides an overview, full details can be found in the actual ITIL publications themselves.

This guide describes the key principles of IT Service Management and provides a high-level overview of each of the core publications within ITIL:

- Service Strategy
- Service Design
- Service Transition
- Service Operation
- Continual Service Improvement.

An overview of the qualifications scheme is also included.

The advice contained within this guide is neither definitive nor prescriptive, but is based on ITIL Best Practice. The guidance in the ITIL publications is applicable generically and is of benefit to all IT organizations irrespective of their size or the technology in use. It is neither bureaucratic nor unwieldy if utilized sensibly and in full recognition of the business needs of the organization.

# Contents

# 1  Introduction

It has become increasingly recognized that information is the most important strategic resource that any organization has to manage. Key to the collection, analysis, production and distribution of information within an organization is the quality of the IT Services provided to the business. It is essential that we recognize that IT Services are crucial, strategic, organizational assets and therefore organizations must invest appropriate levels of resource into the support, delivery and management of these critical IT Services and the IT systems that underpin them. However, these aspects of IT are often overlooked or only superficially addressed within many organizations.

Key issues facing many of today's senior Business Managers and IT Managers are:

- IT and business strategic planning
- Integrating and aligning IT and business goals
- Implementing continual improvement
- Measuring IT organization effectiveness and efficiency
- Optimizing costs and the Total Cost of Ownership (TCO)
- Achieving and demonstrating Return on Investment (ROI)
- Demonstrating the business value of IT
- Developing business and IT partnerships and relationships
- Improving project delivery success
- Outsourcing, insourcing and smart sourcing
- Using IT to gain competitive advantage
- Delivering the required, business justified IT services (i.e. what is required, when required and at an agreed cost)
- Managing constant business and IT change
- Demonstrating appropriate IT governance.

The challenges for IT managers are to co-ordinate and work in partnership with the business to deliver high quality IT services. This has to be achieved while adopting a more business and customer oriented approach to delivering services and cost optimization.

The primary objective of Service Management is to ensure that the IT services are aligned to the business needs and actively support them. It is imperative that the IT services underpin the business processes, but it is also increasingly important that IT acts as an agent for change to facilitate business transformation.

All organizations that use IT depend on IT to be successful. If IT processes and IT services are implemented, managed and supported in the appropriate way, the business will be more successful, suffer less disruption and loss of productive hours, reduce costs, increase revenue, improve public relations and achieve its business objectives.

Key sections within this guide:

- Section 4 overviews Service Strategy: The achievement of strategic goals or objectives requires the use of strategic assets. The guidance shows how to transform service management into a strategic asset.

- Section 5 overviews Service Design: guidance on designing IT services, along with the governing IT practices, processes and policies, to realize the strategy and facilitate the introduction of services into the live environment ensuring quality service delivery, customer satisfaction and cost-effective service provision.

- Section 6 overviews Service Transition: guidance for the development of capabilities for transitioning new and changed services into operations, ensuring the requirements of Service Strategy, encoded in Service Design, are effectively realized in Service Operations while controlling the risks of failure and disruption.

- Section 7 overviews Service Operation: guidance on achieving effectiveness and efficiency in the delivery and support of services to ensure value for the customer and the service provider. Strategic objectives are ultimately realized through Service Operations.

- Section 8 overviews Continual Service Improvement: guidance in creating and maintaining value for customers through better design, introduction and operation of services, linking improvement efforts and outcomes with Service Strategy, Design, Transition and Operation.

- Section 10 Qualifications provides an outline of the current and proposed qualification scheme.

# What is IT Service Management

To understand what service management is, we need to understand what services are, and how service management can help service providers to deliver and manage these services.

*A service is a means of delivering value to customers by facilitating outcomes customers want to achieve without the ownership of specific costs and risks.*

A simple example of a customer outcome that could be facilitated by an IT service might be: "Sales people spending more time interacting with customers" facilitated by "a remote access service that enables reliable access to corporate sales systems from sales people's laptops".

The outcomes that customers want to achieve are the reason why they purchase or use the service. The value of the service to the customer is directly dependent on how well it facilitates these outcomes. Service management is what enables a service provider to understand the services they are providing, to ensure that the services really do facilitate the outcomes their customers want to achieve, to understand the value of the services to their customers, and to understand and manage all of the costs and risks associated with those services.

*Service Management is a set of specialized organizational capabilities for providing value to customers in the form of services.*

These "specialized organizational capabilities" are described in this pocket guide. They include all of the processes, methods, functions, roles and activities that a Service Provider uses to enable them to deliver services to their customers.

Service management is concerned with more than just delivering services. Each service, process or infrastructure component has a lifecycle, and service management considers the entire lifecycle from strategy through design and transition to operation and continual improvement.

The inputs to service management are the resources and capabilities that represent the assets of the service provider. The outputs are the services that provide value to the customers.

Effective service management is itself a strategic asset of the service provider, providing them with the ability to carry out their core business of providing services that deliver value to customers by facilitating the outcomes customers want to achieve.

Adopting good practice can help a service provider to create an effective service management system. Good practice is simply doing things that have been shown to work and to be effective. Good practice can come from many different sources, including public frameworks (such as ITIL, COBIT and CMMI), standards (such as ISO/IEC 20000 and ISO 9000), and proprietary knowledge of people and organizations.

# 3 What is ITIL?

ITIL is a public framework that describes Best Practice in IT service management. It provides a framework for the governance of IT, the 'service wrap', and focuses on the continual measurement and improvement of the quality of IT service delivered, from both a business and a customer perspective. This focus is a major factor in ITIL's worldwide success and has contributed to its prolific usage and to the key benefits obtained by those organizations deploying the techniques and processes throughout their organizations. Some of these benefits include:

- increased user and customer satisfaction with IT services

- improved service availability, directly leading to increased business profits and revenue

- financial savings from reduced rework, lost time, improved resource management and usage

- improved time to market for new products and services

- improved decision making and optimized risk.

ITIL was published between 1989 and 1995 by Her Majesty's Stationery Office (HMSO) in the UK on behalf of the Central Communications and Telecommunications Agency (CCTA) – now subsumed within the Office of Government Commerce (OGC). Its early use was principally confined to the UK and Netherlands. A second version of ITIL was published as a set of revised books between 2000 and 2004.

The initial version of ITIL consisted of a library of 31 associated books covering all aspects of IT service provision. This initial version was then revised and replaced by seven, more closely connected and consistent books (ITIL V2) consolidated within an overall framework. This second version became universally accepted and is now used in many countries by thousands of organizations as the basis for effective IT service provision. In 2007, ITIL V2 was superseded by an enhanced and consolidated third version of ITIL, consisting of five core books covering the service lifecycle, together with the Official Introduction.

The five core books cover each stage of the service lifecycle (Figure 1), from the initial definition and analysis of business requirements in Service Strategy and Service Design, through migration into the live environment within Service Transition, to live operation and improvement in Service Operation and Continual Service Improvement.

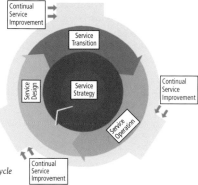

*Figure 1: The service lifecycle*

The five books are described in more detail in the following sections of this pocket guide. A sixth book, the Official Introduction, offers an overview of the five books and an introduction to IT Service Management as a whole.

The core books are the starting point for ITIL V3. It is intended that the content of these core books will be enhanced by additional complementary publications and by a set of supporting web services (Figure 2). In addition, the ITIL V3 Process Model will be made available via the www.itil-live-portal.com website.

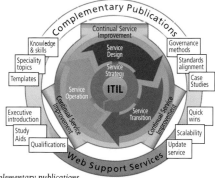

*Figure 2: Complementary publications*

These additional sources of information will provide:

- knowledge and skills: information on the experience and knowledge needed to exploit (and gained through) ITIL

- speciality topics: specific areas of interest, such as outsourcing

- templates

- governance methods: details of methods that have been successfully used to govern Service Management systems and activities

- standards alignment: information on the alignment of ITIL with international standards

- executive introduction: introductory guides for executives and senior managers on the benefits and value of using ITIL

- study aids: additional guides that can be used by students studying ITIL, particularly on accredited training courses

- qualifications: a set of qualifications based around the core publications and their use within the industry

- quick wins: details of potential quick wins and benefits that can be obtained from the adoption of ITIL practices

- scalability: how to scale service management implementation for specific organizations, such as very small or very large businesses

- update service: a web-based service providing regular updates on the progress and ongoing development of ITIL.

All service solutions and activities should be driven by business needs and requirements. Within this context they must also reflect the strategies and policies of the service provider organization, as indicated in Figure 3.

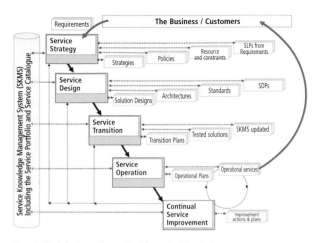

*Figure 3: Key links, inputs & outputs of the service lifecycle stages*

The diagram illustrates how the service lifecycle is initiated from a change in requirements in the business.

These requirements are identified and agreed within the Service Strategy stage within a Service Level Package (SLP) and a defined set of business outcomes.

This passes to the Service Design stage where a service solution is produced together with a Service Design Package (SDP) containing everything necessary to take this service through the remaining stages of the lifecycle.

The SDP passes to the Service Transition stage, where the service is evaluated, tested and validated, the Service Knowledge Management System (SKMS) is updated, and the service is transitioned into the live environment, where it enters the Service Operation stage.

Wherever possible, Continual Service Improvement identifies opportunities for the improvement of weaknesses or failures anywhere within any of the lifecycle stages.

# 4 Service Strategy

## Purpose

The service strategy of any service provider must be grounded upon a fundamental acknowledgement that its customers do not buy products, they buy the satisfaction of particular needs. Therefore, to be successful, the services provided must be perceived by the customer to deliver sufficient value in the form of outcomes that the customer wants to achieve.

Achieving a deep understanding of customer needs, in terms of what these needs are, and when and why they occur, also requires a clear understanding of exactly who is an existing or potential customer of that service provider. This, in turn, requires the service provider to understand the wider context of the current and potential market places that the service provider operates in, or may wish to operate in.

A service strategy can not be created or exist in isolation of the over-arching strategy and culture of the organization that the service provider belongs to. The service provider may exist within an organization solely to deliver service to one specific business unit, to service multiple business units, or may operate as an external service provider serving multiple external businesses. The strategy adopted must provide sufficient value to the customers and all of the service provider's stakeholders – it must fulfill the service provider's strategic purpose.

Irrespective of the context in which the service provider operates, its service strategy must also be based upon a clear recognition of the existence of competition, an awareness that each side has choices, and a view of how that service provider will differentiate itself from the competition. All providers need a service strategy.

Hence, the Service Strategy publication sits at the core of the ITIL V3 lifecycle. It sets out guidance to all IT service providers and their customers, to help them operate and thrive in the long term by building a clear service strategy, i.e. a precise understanding of:

- what services should be offered
- who the services should be offered to

- how the internal and external market places for their services should be developed

- the existing and potential competition in these marketplaces, and the objectives that will differentiate the value of what you do or how you do it

- how the customer(s) and stakeholders will perceive and measure value, and how this value will be created

- how customers will make service sourcing decisions with respect to use of different types of service providers

- how visibility and control over value creation will be achieved through financial management

- how robust business cases will be created to secure strategic investment in service assets and service management capabilities

- how the allocation of available resources will be tuned to optimal effect across the portfolio of services

- how service performance will be measured.

## Key Concepts
The Service Strategy publication defines some key ITIL concepts.

### The four Ps of Strategy:

- *perspective:* the distinctive vision and direction

- *position:* the basis on which the provider will compete

- *plan:* how the provider will achieve their vision

- *pattern:* the fundamental way of doing things – distinctive patterns in decisions and actions over time.

### Competition and Market Space:

- every service provider is subject to competitive forces

- all service providers and customers operate in one or more internal or external market spaces. The service provider must strive to achieve a better understanding than its competitors of the dynamics of the market space, its customers within it, and the combination of critical success factors that are unique to that market space.

***Service Value:*** defined in terms of the customer's perceived business outcomes, and described in terms of the combination of two components:

- ***Service Utility:*** what the customer gets in terms of outcomes supported and/or constraints removed
- ***Service Warranty:*** how the service is delivered and its fitness for use, in terms of availability, capacity, continuity and security.

Service Value also includes the associated concepts of services as Assets, Value Networks, Value Creation and Value Capture.

***Service Provider Types:***

- ***Type I:*** exists within an organization solely to deliver service to one specific business unit
- ***Type II:*** services multiple business units in the same organization
- ***Type III:*** operates as an external service provider serving multiple external customers.

***Service Management as a Strategic Asset:*** the use of ITIL to transform service management capabilities into strategic assets, by using Service Management to provide the basis for core competency, distinctive performance and durable advantage, and increase the service provider's potential from their:

- *capabilities:* the provider's ability (in terms of management, organization, processes, knowledge and people) to coordinate, control and deploy resources
- *resources:* the direct inputs for the production of services, e.g. financial, capital, infrastructure, applications, information and people.

***Critical Success Factors (CSFs):*** the identification, measurement and periodic review of CSFs to determine the service assets required to successfully implement the desired service strategy.

***Service Oriented Accounting:*** using financial management to understand services in terms of consumption and provisioning, and achieve translation between corporate financial systems and service management.

*Service Provisioning Models:* categorization and analysis of the various models that may be selected by customers and used by service providers to source and deliver services, and the financial management impacts of on-shore, off-shore or near-shore variants:

- *Managed Service:* where a business unit requiring a service fully funds the provision of that service for itself
- *Shared Service:* the provisioning of multiple services to one or more business units through shared infrastructure and resources
- *Utility:* services are provided on the basis of how much is required by each customer, how often, and at what times the customer needs them.

*Organization Design and Development:* achieving an ongoing shape and structure to the service provider's organization that enables the service strategy. Considerations include:

- Organizational Development Stages: delivering services through network, direction, delegation, coordination or collaboration depending on the evolutionary state of the organization
- Sourcing Strategy: making informed decisions on service sourcing in terms of internal services, shared services, full service outsourcing, prime consortium or selective outsourcing
- Service Analytics: using technology to help achieve an understanding of the performance of a service through analysis
- Service Interfaces: the mechanisms by which users and other processes interact with each service
- Risk Management: mapping and managing the portfolio of risks underlying a service portfolio.

## Key Processes and Activities

In addition to Strategy Generation, Service Strategy also includes the following key processes.

### Financial Management

Financial Management covers the function and processes responsible for managing an IT service provider's budgeting, accounting and charging requirements. It provides the business and IT with the quantification, in financial terms, of the value of IT services, the value of the assets underlying the provisioning of those services, and the qualification of operational forecasting.

IT Financial Management responsibilities and activities do not exist solely within the IT finance and accounting domain. Many parts of the organization interact to generate and use IT financial information; aggregating, sharing and maintaining the financial data they need, enabling the dissemination of information to feed critical decisions and activities.

## Service Portfolio Management (SPM)

SPM involves proactive management of the investment across the service lifecycle, including those services in the concept, design and transition pipeline, as well as live services defined in the various service catalogues and retired services.

SPM is an ongoing process, which includes the following:

- Define: inventory services, ensure business cases and validate portfolio data

- Analyze: maximize portfolio value, align and prioritize and balance supply and demand

- Approve: finalize proposed portfolio, authorize services and resources

- Charter: communicate decisions, allocate resources and charter services.

## Demand Management

Demand management is a critical aspect of service management. Poorly managed demand is a source of risk for service providers because of uncertainty in demand. Excess capacity generates cost without creating value that provides a basis for cost recovery.

The purpose of Demand Management is to understand and influence customer demand for services and the provision of capacity to meet these demands. At a strategic level this can involve analysis of patterns of business activity and user profiles. At a tactical level it can involve use of differential charging to encourage customers to use IT services at less busy times.

A Service Level Package (SLP) defines the level of utility and warranty for a Service Package and is designed to meet the needs of a pattern of business activity.

## Key Roles and Responsibilities

The Service Strategy publication defines some specific roles and responsibilities associated with the execution of a successful service strategy, including:

- Business Relationship Manager (BRM): BRMs establish a strong business relationship with the customer by understanding the customer's business and their customer outcomes. BRMs work closely with the Product Managers to negotiate productive capacity on behalf of customers.

- Product Manager (PM): PMs take responsibility for developing and managing services across the life-cycle, and have responsibilities for productive capacity,   service pipeline, and the services, solutions and packages that are presented in the service catalogues.

- Chief Sourcing Officer (CSO): the CSO is the champion of the sourcing strategy within the organization, responsible for leading and directing the sourcing office and development of the sourcing strategy in close conjunction with the CIO.

# 5 Service Design

## Purpose

Service Design is a stage within the overall service lifecycle and an important element within the business change process. The role of Service Design within the business change process can be defined as:

*The design of appropriate and innovative IT services, including their architectures, processes, policies and documentation, to meet current and future agreed business requirements.*

The main goals and objectives of Service Design are to:

- design services to meet agreed business outcomes
- design processes to support the service lifecycle
- identify and manage risks
- design secure and resilient IT infrastructures, environments, applications and data/information resources and capability
- design measurement methods and metrics
- produce and maintain plans, processes, policies, standards, architectures, frameworks and documents to support the design of quality IT solutions
- develop skills and capability within IT
- contribute to the overall improvement in IT service quality.

## Key Principles

Service Design starts with a set of business requirements, and ends with the development of a service solution designed to meet documented business requirements and outcomes and to provide a Service Design Package (SDP) for handover into Service Transition.

There are *5 individual aspects of Service Design*:

- new or changed service solutions
- service management systems and tools, especially the Service Portfolio
- technology architectures and management systems
- processes, roles and capabilities
- measurement methods and metrics.

A holistic approach should be adopted in Service Design to ensure consistency and integration in all IT activities and processes, providing end-to-end business-related functionality and quality. Good service design is dependent upon the effective and efficient use of the ***Four Ps of Design***:

- *people:* the people, skills and competencies involved in the provision of IT services

- *products:* the technology and management systems used in the delivery of IT services

- *processes:* the processes, roles and activities involved in the provision of IT services

- *partners:* the vendors, manufacturers and suppliers used to assist and support IT service provision.

***Service Design Package (SDP):*** defines all aspects of an IT service and its requirements through each stage of its lifecycle. An SDP is produced for each new IT service, major change, or IT service retirement.

## Key Processes and Activities
### Service Catalogue Management (SCM)
The Service Catalogue provides a central source of information on the IT services delivered to the business by the service provider organization, ensuring that business areas can view an accurate, consistent picture of the IT services available, their details and status.

The purpose of Service Catalogue Management (SCM) is to provide a single, consistent source of information on all of the agreed services, and ensure that it is widely available to those who are approved to access it.

The key information within the SCM process is that contained within the Service Catalogue. The main input for this information comes from the Service Portfolio and the business via either the Business Relationship Management or the Service Level Management processes.

### Service Level Management (SLM)
SLM negotiates, agrees and documents appropriate IT service targets with the business, and then monitors and produces reports on delivery against the agreed level of service.

The purpose of the SLM process is to ensure that all operational services and their performance are measured in a consistent, professional manner throughout the IT organization, and that the services and the reports produced meet the needs of the business and customers.

The main information provided by the SLM process includes Service Level Agreements (SLA), Operational Level Agreements (OLA) and other support agreements, and the production of the Service Improvement Plan (SIP) and the Service Quality Plan.

### Capacity Management

Capacity Management includes business, service and component capacity management across the service lifecycle. A key success factor in managing capacity is ensuring that it is considered during the design stage.

The purpose of Capacity Management is to provide a point of focus and management for all capacity and performance-related issues, relating to both services and resources, and to match the capacity of IT to the agreed business demands.

The Capacity Management Information System (CMIS) is the cornerstone of a successful Capacity Management process. Information contained within the CMIS is stored and analyzed by all the sub-processes of Capacity Management for the provision of technical and management reports, including the Capacity Plan.

### Availability Management

The purpose of Availability Management is to provide a point of focus and management for all availability-related issues, relating to services, components and resources, ensuring that availability targets in all areas are measured and achieved, and that they match or exceed the current and future agreed needs of the business in a cost-effective manner.

Availability Management should take place at two inter-connected levels and aim to continually optimize and proactively improve the availability of IT services and their supporting organization. There are two key aspects:

■ *reactive activities:* monitoring, measuring, analysis and management of events, incidents and problems involving service unavailability

■ *proactive activities:* proactive planning, design, recommendation and improvement of availability.

Availability Management activities should consider the availability, reliability, maintainability and serviceability at both service and component level, particularly those supporting Vital Business Functions (VBFs).

The Availability Management process should be based around an Information System (AMIS) that contains all of the measurements and information required to provide the appropriate information to the business on service levels. The AMIS also assists in the production of the Availability Plan.

### IT Service Continuity Management (ITSCM)

As technology is a core component of most business processes, continued or high availability of IT is critical to the survival of the business as a whole. This is achieved by introducing risk reduction measures and recovery options. On-going maintenance of the recovery capability is essential if it is to remain effective.

The purpose of ITSCM is to maintain the appropriate on-going recovery capability within IT services to match the agreed needs, requirements and timescales of the business.

ITSCM includes a series of activities throughout the lifecycle to ensure that, once service continuity and recovery plans have been developed, they are kept aligned with Business Continuity Plans and business priorities.

The maintenance of appropriate ITSCM policy strategies and ITSCM plans aligned with business plans is key to the success of an ITSCM process. This can be accomplished by the regular completion of Business Impact Analysis and Risk Management exercises.

### Information Security Management (ISM)

ISM needs to be considered within the overall corporate governance framework. Corporate governance is the set of responsibilities and practices exercised by the board and executive management with the goal of providing strategic direction, ensuring that the objectives are achieved, ascertaining that the risks are being managed appropriately, and verifying that the enterprise's resources are used effectively.

The purpose of the ISM process is to align IT security with business security and ensure that information security is effectively managed in all service and Service Management activities, such that:

- information is available and usable when required (availability)
- information is observed by or disclosed to only those who have a right to know (confidentiality)
- information is complete, accurate and protected against unauthorized modification (integrity)
- business transactions, as well as information exchanges, can be trusted (authenticity and non-repudiation).

ISM should maintain and enforce an overall policy, together with a set of supporting controls within an integrated Security Management Information System (SMIS), aligned with business security policies and strategies.

### Supplier Management
The Supplier Management process ensures that suppliers and the services they provide are managed to support IT service targets and business expectations.

The purpose of the Supplier Management process is to obtain value for money from suppliers and to ensure that suppliers perform to the targets contained within their contracts and agreements, while conforming to all of the terms and conditions.

The Supplier and Contract Database (SCD) is a vital source of information on suppliers and contracts and should contain all of the information necessary for the management of suppliers, contracts and their associated services.

### Key Service Design stage activities
- Business requirements collection, analysis and engineering to ensure they are clearly documented.
- Design and development of appropriate service solutions, technology, processes, information and measurements.
- Production and revision of all design processes and documents involved in Service Design.
- Liaison with all other design and planning activities and roles.

- Production and maintenance of policies and design documents.

- Risk management of all services and design processes.

- Alignment with all corporate and IT strategies and policies.

## Key Roles and Responsibilities

The key roles involved within the Service Design activities and processes are:

- Service Design Manager: responsible for the overall coordination and deployment of quality solution designs for services and processes

- IT Designer/Architect: responsible for the overall coordination and design of the required technologies, architectures, strategies, designs and plans

- Service Catalogue Manager: responsible for producing and maintaining an accurate Service Catalogue

- Service Level Manager: responsible for ensuring that the service quality levels are agreed and met

- Availability Manager: responsible for ensuring that all services meet their agreed availability targets

- IT Service Continuity Manager: responsible for ensuring that all services can be recovered in line with their agreed business needs, requirements and timescales

- Capacity Manager: responsible for ensuring that IT capacity is matched to agreed current and future business demands

- Security Manager: responsible for ensuring that IT security is aligned with agreed business security policy risks, impacts and requirements

- Supplier Manager: responsible for ensuring that value for money is obtained from all IT suppliers and contracts, and that underpinning contracts and agreements are aligned with the needs of the business.

# 6 Service Transition

## Purpose

The role of Service Transition is to deliver services that are required by the business into operational use. Service Transition delivers this by receiving the Service Design Package from the Service Design stage and delivering into the Operational stage every necessary element required for ongoing operation and support of that service. If business circumstances, assumptions or requirements have changed since design, then modifications may well be required during the Service Transition stage in order to deliver the required service.

Service Transition focuses on implementing all aspects of the service, not just the application and how it is used in 'normal' circumstances. It needs to ensure that the service can operate in foreseeable extreme or abnormal circumstances, and that support for failure or errors is available. This requires sufficient understanding of:

- potential business value and who it is delivered to/judged by
- identification of all stakeholders within supplier, customer and other areas
- application and adaptation of service design, including arranging for modification of the design, where the need is detected during transition.

## Key Principles

Service Transition is supported by underlying principles that facilitate effective and efficient use of new/changed services. Key principles include:

- Understanding all services, their utility and warranties - to transition a service effectively it is essential to know its nature and purpose in terms of the outcomes and/or removed business constraints (utilities) and the assurances that the utilities will be delivered (warranties).
- Establishing a formal policy and common framework for implementation of all required changes - consistency and comprehensiveness ensure that no services, stakeholders, occasions etc. are missed out and so cause service failures.
- Supporting knowledge transfer, decision support and re-use of processes, systems and other elements – effective Service Transition is delivered by involving all relevant parties, ensuring appropriate knowledge is available and that work done is reusable in future similar circumstances.

- Anticipating and managing 'course corrections' – being proactive and determining likely course correction requirements, and when elements of a service do need to be adjusted, this is undertaken logically and is fully documented.
- Ensuring involvement of Service Transition and Service Transition requirements throughout the service lifecycle.

## Key Processes and Activities

Within the Service Transition process set, some of the processes most important to Service Transition are whole lifecycle processes and have impact, input and monitoring and control considerations across all lifecycle stages. The whole lifecycle processes are:

- Change Management
- Service Asset and Configuration Management
- Knowledge Management.

Processes focused on Service Transition, but not exclusive to the stage, are:

- Transition Planning and Support
- Release and Deployment Management
- Service Validation and Testing
- Evaluation.

## Change Management

Change Management ensures that changes are recorded, evaluated, authorized, prioritized, planned, tested, implemented, documented and reviewed in a controlled manner.

The purpose of the Change Management process is to ensure that standardized methods are used for the efficient and prompt handling of all changes, that all changes are recorded in the Configuration Management System and that overall business risk is optimized.

The process addresses all service change.

*A Service Change is the addition, modification or removal of an authorised, planned or supported service or service component and its associated documentation.*

Therefore change management is relevant across the whole lifecycle, applying to all levels of service management – strategic, tactical and operational.

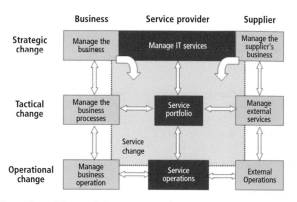

*Figure 4: Scope of change and release management for services*

Change management delivers, to the business, reduced errors in new or changed services and faster, more accurate implementation of changes; it allows restricted funds and resources to be focused on those changes to achieve greatest benefit to the business.

### Service Asset and Configuration Management (SACM)

SACM supports the business by providing accurate information and control across all assets and relationships that make up an organization's infrastructure.

The purpose of SACM is to identify, control and account for service assets and configuration items (CI), protecting and ensuring their integrity across the service lifecycle.

The scope of SACM also extends to non-IT assets and to internal and external service providers, where shared assets need to be controlled.

To manage large and complex IT services and infrastructures, SACM requires the use of a supporting system known as the Configuration Management System (CMS).

## Knowledge Management

The purpose of Knowledge Management is to ensure that the right person has the right knowledge, at the right time to deliver and support the services required by the business. This delivers:

- more efficient services with improved quality
- clear and common understanding of the value provided by services
- relevant information that is always available.

At the heart of Knowledge Management is the Data-Information-Knowledge-Wisdom structure, condensing raw – and unusable – data into valuable assets. This is illustrated by the Service Knowledge Management System, holding relevant information and wisdom derived from Asset and Configuration Data.

## Transition Planning and Support

The goals of Transition Planning and Support are to:

- plan and coordinate resources to ensure that the requirements of Service Strategy encoded in Service Design are effectively realized in Service Operations
- identify, manage and control the risks of failure and disruption across transition activities.

Effective Transition Planning and Support can significantly improve a service provider's ability to handle high volumes of change and releases across its customer base.

## Release and Deployment Management

The goal of the Release and Deployment Management process is to assemble and position all aspects of services into production and establish effective use of new or changed services.

Effective release and deployment delivers significant business value by delivering changes at optimized speed, risk and cost, and offering a consistent, appropriate and auditable implementation of usable and useful business services.

Release and Deployment Management covers the whole assembly and implementation of new/changed services for operational use, from release planning through to early life support.

## Service Validation and Testing

Successful testing depends on understanding the service holistically – how it will be used and the way it is constructed. All services – whether in-house or bought-in – will need to be tested appropriately, providing validation that business requirements can be met in the full range of expected situations, to the extent of agreed business risk.

The key purpose of service validation and testing is to provide objective evidence that the new/changed service supports the business requirements, including the agreed SLAs.

The service is tested explicitly against the utilities and warranties set out in the service design package, including business functionality, availability, continuity, security, usability and regression testing.

## Evaluation

Ensuring that the service will be useful to the business is central to successful Service Transition and this extends into ensuring that the service will continue to be relevant by establishing appropriate metrics and measurement techniques.

Evaluation considers the input to Service Transition, addressing the relevance of the service design, the transition approach itself, and the suitability of the new or changed service for the actual operational and business environments encountered and expected.

## Service Transition Stage Operational Activities

Service Transition is also the focus for some operational activities. These have wider applicability than Service Transition and comprise:

- managing communications and commitment across IT Service Management
- managing organizational and stakeholder change
- stakeholder management
- organization of Service Transition and key roles.

## Key Roles and Responsibilities

The staff delivering Service Transition within an organization must be organized for effectiveness and efficiency, and various options exist to deliver this. It is not anticipated that a typical organization would consider a separate group of people for this role, rather there is a flow of experience and skills – meaning the same people may well be involved in multiple lifecycle stages.

# 7 Service Operation

## Purpose

The purpose of Service Operation is to deliver agreed levels of service to users and customers, and to manage the applications, technology and infrastructure that support delivery of the services.

It is only during this stage of the lifecycle that services actually deliver value to the business, and it is the responsibility of Service Operation staff to ensure that this value is delivered.

It is important for Service Operation to balance conflicting goals:

- internal IT view versus external business view
- stability versus responsiveness
- quality of service versus cost of service
- reactive versus proactive activities.

For each of these conflicts, staff must maintain an even balance, as excessive focus on one side of any of these will result in poor service.

Many organizations find it helpful to consider the "operational health" of services. This identifies "vital signs" that are critical for execution of Vital Business Functions. If these are within normal ranges, the system or service is healthy. This leads to a reduction in the cost of monitoring, and enables staff to focus on areas that will lead to service success.

## Key processes and activities

### Event Management Process

*An event is a change of state that has significance for the management of a configuration item or IT service.*

An event may indicate that something is not functioning correctly, leading to an incident being logged. Events may also indicate normal activity, or a need for routine intervention such as changing a tape.

Event management depends on monitoring, but it is different. Event management generates and detects notifications, whilst monitoring checks the status of components even when no events are occurring.

Events may be detected by a CI sending a message, or by a management tool polling the CI. After an event has been detected it may lead to an Incident, Problem or Change, or it may simply be logged in case the information is needed.

Response to an event may be automated or may require manual intervention. If actions are needed then a trigger, such as an SMS message or an incident being automatically logged, can alert support staff.

## Incident Management Process
*An incident is an unplanned interruption to an IT service, or a reduction in the quality of an IT service. Failure of a configuration item that has not yet impacted service is also an incident.*

The purpose of Incident Management is to restore normal service as quickly as possible, and to minimize the adverse impact on business operations.

Incidents are often detected by event management, or by users contacting the service desk. Incidents are categorized to identify who should work on them and for trend analysis, and they are prioritized according to urgency and business impact.

If an incident cannot be resolved quickly, it may be escalated. Functional escalation passes the incident to a technical support team with appropriate skills; hierarchical escalation engages appropriate levels of management.

After the incident has been investigated and diagnosed, and the resolution has been tested, the Service Desk should ensure that the user is satisfied before the incident is closed.

An Incident Management tool is essential for recording and managing incident information.

## Request Fulfillment Process
*A service request is a request from a user for information or advice, or for a standard change, or for access to an IT service.*

The purpose of Request Fulfillment is to enable users to request and receive standard services; to source and deliver these services; to provide information to users and customers about services and procedures for obtaining them; and to assist with general information, complaints and comments.

All requests should be logged and tracked. The process should include appropriate approval before fulfilling the request.

### Access Management Process

The purpose of the Access Management process is to provide the rights for users to be able to access a service or group of services, while preventing access to non-authorized users.

Access Management helps to manage confidentiality, availability and integrity of data and intellectual property.

Access Management is concerned with identity (unique information that distinguishes an individual) and rights (settings that provide access to data and services). The process includes verifying identity and entitlement, granting access to services, logging and tracking access, and removing or modifying rights when status or roles change.

### Problem Management Process

*A problem is a cause of one or more incidents. The cause is not usually known at the time a problem record is created, and the problem management process is responsible for further investigation.*

The key objectives of Problem Management are to prevent problems and resulting incidents from happening, to eliminate recurring incidents and to minimize the impact of incidents that cannot be prevented.

Problem Management includes diagnosing causes of incidents, determining the resolution, and ensuring that the resolution is implemented.  Problem Management also maintains information about problems and the appropriate workarounds and resolutions.

Problems are categorized in a similar way to incidents, but the goal is to understand causes, document workarounds and request changes to permanently resolve the problems. Workarounds are documented in a Known Error Database, which improves the efficiency and effectiveness of Incident Management.

## *Common Service Operation Activities*
Service Operation includes a number of activities that are not part of the five processes described. These include:

- monitoring and control: to detect the status of services and CIs and take appropriate corrective action
- console management/operations bridge: a central coordination point for monitoring and managing services
- management of the infrastructure: storage, databases, middleware, directory services, facilities/data centre etc.
- operational aspects of processes from other lifecycle stages: Change, Configuration, Release and Deployment, Availability, Capacity, Knowledge, Service Continuity Management etc.

## Key Functions

### *Service Desk Function*
The Service Desk provides a single central point of contact for all users of IT. The Service Desk usually logs and manages all incidents, service requests and access requests and provides an interface for all other Service Operation processes and activities.

Specific Service Desk responsibilities include:

- logging all incidents and requests, categorizing and prioritizing them
- first-line investigation and diagnosis
- managing the lifecycle of incidents and requests, escalating as appropriate and closing them when the user is satisfied
- keeping users informed of the status of services, incidents and requests.

There are many ways of structuring and organizing service desks, including:

- local service desk: physically close to the users
- centralized service desk: allows fewer staff to deal with a higher volume of calls

- virtual service desk: staff are in many locations but appear to the users to be a single team

- follow the sun: Service Desks in different time zones give 24-hour coverage by passing calls to a location where staff are working.

## Technical Management Function

Technical Management includes all the people who provide technical expertise and management of the IT infrastructure.

Technical Management helps to plan, implement and maintain a stable technical infrastructure and ensure that required resources and expertise are in place to design, build, transition, operate and improve the IT services and supporting technology.

Activities carried out by Technical Management include:

- identifying knowledge and expertise requirements

- defining architecture standards

- involvement in the design and build of new services and operational practices

- contributing to service design, service transition or continual service improvement projects

- assistance with service management processes, helping to define standards and tools, and undertaking activities such as the evaluation of change requests

- assistance with the management of contracts and vendors.

Technical Management is usually organized based on the infrastructure that each team supports.

## Application Management Function

Application Management includes all the people who provide technical expertise and management of applications. As such they carry out a very similar role to Technical Management, but with a focus on software applications rather than infrastructure.

It is common in many organizations to refer to applications as services, but applications are just one component needed to provide a service. Each application may support more than one service, and each service may make use of many applications. This is especially true for modern service providers who create shared services based on service- oriented architectures.

Application Management works closely with Development, but is a distinct function with different roles. Activities carried out by Application Management are similar to those described above for Technical Management.

Application Management is usually organized by the lines of business that each team supports.

### IT Operations Management Function
IT Operations Management is responsible for the management and maintenance of the IT infrastructure required to deliver the agreed level of IT services to the business. It includes two functions:

- IT Operations Control is usually staffed by shifts of operators who carry out routine operational tasks. They provide centralized monitoring and control, usually from an operations bridge or network operations centre.

- Facilities Management is responsible for management of data centres, computer rooms and recovery sites. Facilities Management also coordinates large-scale projects, such as data centre consolidation or server consolidation.

## Purpose

Continual Service Improvement (CSI) is concerned with maintaining value for customers through the continual evaluation and improvement of the quality of services and the overall maturity of the ITSM service lifecycle and underlying processes.

CSI combines principles, practices and methods from quality management, Change Management and capability improvement, working to improve each stage in the service lifecycle, as well as the current services, processes, and related activities and technology.

CSI is not a new concept, but for most organizations the concept has not moved beyond the discussion stage. For many organizations, CSI becomes a project when something has failed and severely impacted the business. When the issue is resolved the concept is promptly forgotten until the next major failure occurs. Discrete time-bound projects are still required, but to be successful CSI must be embedded within the organizational culture and become a routine activity.

The CSI Model shown in Figure 5 provides a way for an organization to identify and manage appropriate improvements by contrasting their current position and the value they are providing to the business, with their long-term goals and objectives, and identifying any gaps that exist. This is done on a continual basis to address changes in business requirements, technology, and to ensure high quality is maintained.

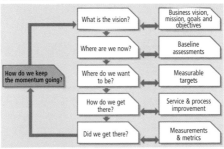

*Figure 5: The Continual Service Improvement Model*

### Key processes and activities

CSI defines three key processes for the effective implementation of continual improvement, the 7-Step Improvement Process, Service Measurement, and Service Reporting.

### 7-Step Improvement Process

The 7-step improvement process covers the steps required to collect meaningful data, analyze this data to identify trends and issues, present the information to management for their prioritization and agreement, and implement improvements.

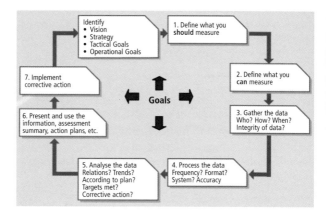

*Figure 6: The 7-Step Improvement Process*

Each step is driven by the strategic, tactical and operational goals defined during Service Strategy and Service Design:

■ *Step 1 - Define what you should measure*

A set of measurements should be defined that fully support the goals of the organization. The focus should be on identifying what is needed to satisfy the goals fully, without considering whether the data is currently available.

■ *Step 2 - Define what you can measure*

Organizations may find that they have limitations on what can actually be measured, but it is useful to recognize that such gaps exist and what risks may be involved as a result.

A gap analysis should be conducted between what is or can be measured today and what is ideally required. The gaps and implications can then be reported to the business, the customers and IT management. It is possible that new tools or customization will be required at some stage.

■ *Step 3 - Gather the data*

This covers monitoring and data collection. A combination of monitoring tools and manual processes should be put in place to collect the data needed for the measurements that have been defined.

Quality is the key objective of monitoring for CSI. Therefore monitoring focuses on the effectiveness of a service, process, tool, organization or CI. The emphasis is on identifying where improvements can be made to the existing level of service, or IT performance, typically by detecting exceptions and resolutions.

CSI is not only interested in exceptions. If a Service Level Agreement is consistently met over time, CSI is also interested in determining whether that level of performance can be sustained at a lower cost or whether it needs to be upgraded to an even better level of performance.

■ *Step 4 - Process the data*

Raw data is processed into the required format, typically providing an end-to-end perspective on the performance of services and/or processes.

Processing the data is an important CSI activity that is often overlooked. While monitoring and collecting data on a single infrastructure component is important, it is key to understand that component's impact on the larger infrastructure and IT service.

- ### Step 5 - Analyze the data

  Data analysis transforms the information into knowledge of the events that are affecting the organization.

  Once the data is processed into information, the results can be analyzed to answer questions such as:

  - Are we meeting targets?
  - Are there any clear trends?
  - Are corrective actions required? What is the cost?

- ### Step 6 - Present and use the Information

  The knowledge gained can now be presented in a format that is easy to understand and allows those receiving the information to make strategic, tactical and operational decisions. The information needs to be provided at the right level and in the right way for the intended audience. It should provide value, note exceptions to service, and highlight any benefits that have been identified during the time period.

  Now more than ever, IT must invest the time to understand specific business goals and translate IT metrics to reflect an impact against these business goals. Often there is a gap between what IT reports and what is of interest to the business.

  Although most reports tend to concentrate on areas of poor performance, good news should be reported as well. A report showing improvement trends is IT services' best marketing vehicle.

- ### Step 7 - Implement corrective action

  The knowledge gained is used to optimize, improve and correct services, processes, and all other supporting activities and technology. The corrective actions required to improve the service should be identified and communicated to the organization.

  CSI will identify many opportunities for improvement and an organization will need to determine priorities based on their goals, and the resources and funding available.

  The 7-Step Improvement Process is continual and loops back to the beginning.

## Service Measurement

There are four basic reasons to monitor and measure, to:

- *validate* previous decisions that have been made
- *direct* activities in order to meet set targets - this is the most prevalent reason for monitoring and measuring
- *justify* that a course of action is required, with factual evidence or proof
- *intervene* at the appropriate point and take corrective action.

Monitoring and measurement underpins CSI and the 7-Step Improvement Process, and is an essential part of being able to manage services and processes, and report value to the business.

Many organizations today measure at the component level, and although this is necessary and valuable, service measurement must go up a level to provide a view of the true customer experience of services being delivered.

There are three types of metrics that an organization needs to collect to support CSI activities as well as other process activities.

- *Technology metrics:* often associated with component and application based metrics such as performance, availability.
- *Process metrics:* captured in the form of Critical Success Factors (CSFs), Key Performance Indicators (KPIs) and activity metrics.
- *Service metrics:* the results of the end-to-end service.
  Component/technology metrics are used to compute the service metrics.

An integrated Service Measurement Framework needs to be put in place that defines and collects the required metrics and raw data, and supports the reporting and interpretation of that data.

## Service Reporting

A significant amount of data is collated and monitored by IT in the daily delivery of quality service to the business, but only a small subset is of real interest and importance to the business. The business likes to see a historical representation of the past period's performance that portrays their experience, but it is more concerned with those historical events that continue to be a threat going forward, and how IT intends to mitigate against such threats.

It is not enough to present reports depicting adherence or otherwise to SLAs. IT needs to build an actionable approach to reporting, i.e. what happened, what IT did, how IT will ensure it doesn't impact again and how IT are working to improve service delivery generally.

A reporting ethos which focuses on the future as strongly as it focuses on the past also provides the means for IT to market its offerings directly aligned to the positive or negative experiences of the business.

## Key Roles and Responsibilities
Whilst a CSI Manager is responsible for the overall CSI activities within an organization, the majority of the detailed improvement related work is carried out within each of the lifecycle stages, processes and activities.

# 9 Process Cross Reference

Each core ITIL publication addresses a stage in the service lifecycle and defines a key set of processes required during that stage.

Figure 7 provides a pictorial representation of the key processes defined by each publication and lifecycle stage. Table 1 provides an alphabetical list of service management processes defined in ITIL and cross-references them to the publication where they are primarily defined and to any other publication where significant further expansion of the process is provided. Most processes play some role during each stage of the lifecycle, but only significant references from the publications are included in Table 1

| Service Management Process | Primary Source | Further Expansion |
|---|---|---|
| 7-Step Improvement Process | CSI | |
| Access Management | SO | |
| Availability Management | SD | CSI |
| Capacity Management | SD | SO, CSI |
| Change Management | ST | |
| Demand Management | SS | SD |
| Evaluation | ST | |
| Event Management | SO | |
| Financial Management | SS | |
| Incident Management | SO | CSI |
| Information Security Management | SD | SO |
| IT Service Continuity Management | SD | CSI |
| Knowledge Management | ST | CSI |
| Problem Management | SO | CSI |
| Release and Deployment Management | ST | SO |
| Request Fulfillment | SO | |
| Service Asset and Configuration Mgmt | ST | SO |
| Service Catalogue Management | SD | SS |
| Service Level Management | SD | CSI |
| Service Measurement | CSI | |
| Service Portfolio Management | SS | SD |
| Service Reporting | CSI | |
| Service Validation and Testing | ST | |
| Strategy Generation | SS | |
| Supplier Management | SD | |
| Transition Planning and Support | ST | |

*Table 1: ITIL V3 Service Management Processes*

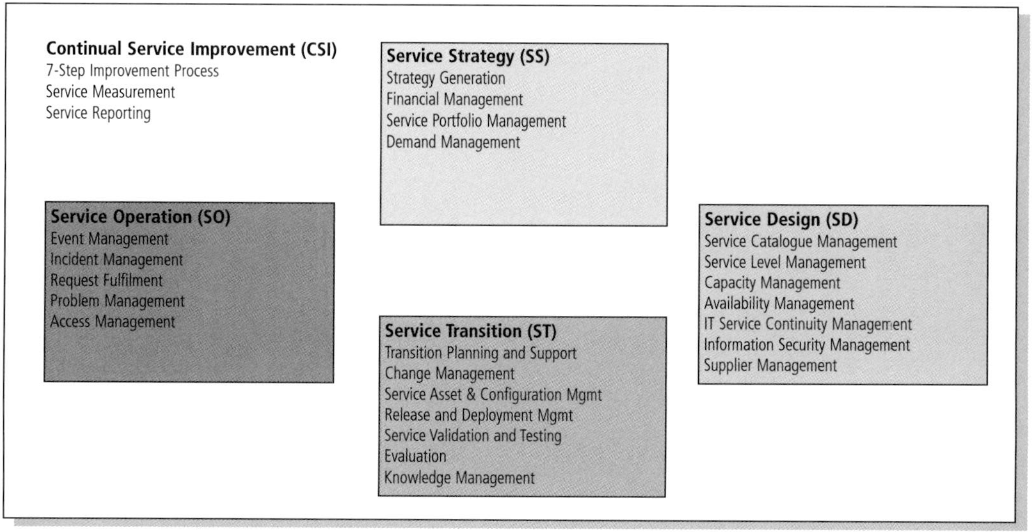

**Continual Service Improvement (CSI)**
7-Step Improvement Process
Service Measurement
Service Reporting

**Service Strategy (SS)**
Strategy Generation
Financial Management
Service Portfolio Management
Demand Management

**Service Design (SD)**
Service Catalogue Management
Service Level Management
Capacity Management
Availability Management
IT Service Continuity Management
Information Security Management
Supplier Management

**Service Transition (ST)**
Transition Planning and Support
Change Management
Service Asset & Configuration Mgmt
Release and Deployment Mgmt
Service Validation and Testing
Evaluation
Knowledge Management

**Service Operation (SO)**
Event Management
Incident Management
Request Fulfilment
Problem Management
Access Management

*Figure 7: ITIL V3 Service Management Processes across the Lifecycle*

# 10 Qualifications

## Overview

The ITIL V3 qualifications scheme introduces a system that starts with the ITIL Foundation for Service Management, and enables an individual to accumulate credits for ITIL V3 courses, leading to an award of the ITIL Diploma in IT Service Management, and ultimately an Advanced Service Management Professional Diploma. (At the time of writing this publication, the precise details of the Advanced Diploma have yet to be finalized. Indeed the whole points/credits system has yet to be finalized and any reference should be treated as provisional )

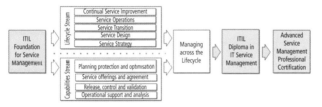

*Figure 8: ITIL V3 qualification scheme*

## Foundation

The Foundation level focuses on knowledge and comprehension to provide a good grounding in the key concepts, terminology and processes of ITIL V3. At this level, the qualification remains very similar to the ITIL V2 Foundation qualification and is achieved through a three-day course including a forty question, one-hour multiple choice examination. Foundation represents 2 credits towards the Diploma.

## Intermediate Streams

To achieve a Diploma, candidates must achieve a total of 22 credits. In addition to the 2 credits from Foundation, candidates gain credits from taking units from either the Lifecycle (3 credits each) or Capabilities (4 credits each) intermediate streams. Both intermediate streams assess an individual's comprehension and application of the concepts of ITIL V3. Candidates may take units from either of the streams. These units give them credits towards a Diploma. The Managing across the Lifecycle course (five credits) is then required to bring together the full essence of a lifecycle approach to service management.

Lifecycle Stream – units based on the five core OGC books:

- Service Strategy

- Service Design

- Service Transition

- Service Operation

- Continual Service Improvement.

Capabilities Stream – units based around four clusters:

- service portfolio and relationship management

- service design and optimization

- service monitoring and control

- service operation and support.

### *Diploma*
Candidates automatically qualify for an ITIL V3 Diploma once they have achieved the pre-requisite 22 credits from Foundation and Intermediate units. No further examination or courses are required.

### *Advanced Service Management Professional Certification*
Although not yet finalized, this qualification is intended to assess an individual's ability to apply and analyze the ITIL V3 concepts in new areas.

## Existing ITIL V1 and V2 Qualifications
The new scheme offers bridging courses and examinations to those candidates with existing ITIL (V1 and V2) qualifications. Candidates with an existing ITIL V1 or V2 Foundation qualification are given 1.5 credits, and successfully passing a V3 Foundation Bridge course provides the further 0.5 credits required to progress into the Intermediate streams.

Candidates with V1 or V2 Manager qualifications are given 17 credits, and successfully passing a V3 Manager Bridge course provides the further 5 credits required to qualify for the ITIL Diploma.

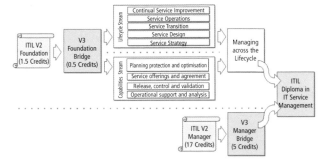

*Figure 9: ITIL V3 bridging qualifications scheme*

## Qualifications Board and Supporting Structure

APM Group is the official Accreditor, and as such is authorized by the OGC to license other Examination Institutes (EIs) to administer ITIL qualification and accreditation activities.

A Global Senior Examiner Panel has been established to:

■ oversee the ongoing development of the qualification structure for ITIL V3

■ design the certification elements required of the scheme

■ produce the requirements for learning objectives and knowledge competency

■ produce the supporting accredited formal syllabi

■ produce the requirements for delivery mechanism

■ produce sample examinations in support of the syllabi

■ provide recommendations on the required trainer and course provider competency to deliver against the scheme

■ manage the exam bank.

This panel consists of the Chief Examiner and the Senior Examiner Panel, and is underpinned by Examination Institutes, the Examiners and Working Groups.

The Accreditor (APMG) licenses the Examination Institutes (EIs). Currently these consist of:

- APMG

- ISEB

- EXIN

- Loyalist College.

These Institutes are in turn underpinned by Accredited Training Organizations (ATOs) that are individually licensed by the EIs.

# 11 Related Standards and Other Sources

ITIL provides advice and guidance on Best Practice relating to the provision of IT services. The following public frameworks and standards are relevant :

- ISO/IEC 20000: IT Service Management
- ISO/IEC 27001: Information Security Management (ISO/IEC 17799 is corresponding Code of Practice)
- Capability Maturity Model Integration (CMMI®)
- Control Objectives for Information and related Technology (COBIT®)
- Projects in Controlled Environments (PRINCE2®)
- Project Management Body of Knowledge (PMBOK®)
- Management of Risk (M_o_R®)
- eSourcing Capability Model for Service Providers (eSCM-SP™)
- Telecom Operations Map (eTOM®)
- Six Sigma™.

Organizations need to integrate guidance from multiple frameworks and standards.

The primary standard for IT Service Management is ISO/IEC 20000. The standard and ITIL are aligned and continue to be aligned, although the standard is currently to be extended with the development of Parts 3 and 4:

- ISO/IEC 20000-1:2005 Part 1: Specification
  Defines the requirements for Service Management
- ISO/IEC 20000-2:2005 Part 2: Code of Practice
  Provides guidance and recommendations on how to meet the requirements in Part 1
- ISO/IEC 20000-3:2007 Part 3: Scoping and applicability (Not available yet)
- ISO/IEC 20000-4:2007 Part 3: Service Management Process Reference Model (Not available yet)
- BIP 0005 : A Manager's Guide to Service Management

- BIP 0015 IT Service Management: Self-assessment Workbook *(currently assesses against ITIL V2, to be revised via ITIL V3 complementary publications).*

These documents provide a standard against which organizations can be assessed and certified with regard to the quality of their IT Service Management processes.

An ISO/IEC 20000 Certification scheme was introduced in December 2005. The scheme was designed by the itSMF UK and is operated under their control. A number of auditing organizations are accredited within the scheme to assess and certify organizations as compliant to the ISO/IEC 20000 standard and its content.

# 12  Summary

Many organizations still see IT service management as being predominantly a technology issue. ITIL promotes a much more "joined up", "end-to-end" approach to IT service management replacing the 'technology silos' and isolated 'islands of excellence'. The focus of IT management has been changing for some time and in the future management will be even less focused on technology and still more integrated with the overall needs of the business management and processes. New management systems are already starting to evolve and will continue to evolve over the next few years. This development will accelerate, as the management standards for the exchange of management information between tools become more fully defined. In essence, management systems will become:

■ more focused on business needs

■ more closely integrated with the business processes

■ less dependent on specific technology and more "service centric"

■ more integrated with other management tools and processes as the management standards evolve.

This will allow "joined up", "end-to-end" IT service management processes to be developed that will replace the 'technical silos' and isolated 'islands of excellence' that have previously existed within IT organizations.

This will only happen if we adopt practices and architectures that are focused on business needs and business processes. The ITIL framework gives a sound basis for achieving all of this once management tools and interfaces evolve to fully support them. Figure 10 illustrates how all of these areas and processes together provide "end-to-end", "joined up" Service Management.

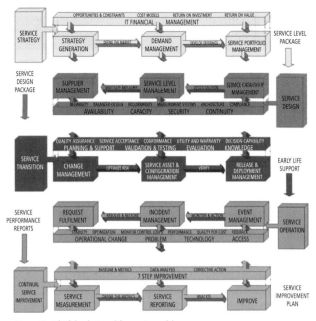

*Figure 10: A high level view of the service model*

Several organizations have already used this approach to significantly improve the quality of IT services delivered to the business. The benefits gained have included:

- Greater alignment of IT services, processes and goals with business requirements, expectations and goals
- Improved business profitability and productivity
- Support staff that are more aware of business processes and business impact
- A reduction in overall management and support costs leading to a reduced TCO
- Improved service availability and performance, leading to increased business revenue
- Improved service levels and quality of service.

# Further Guidance and Contact Points

itSMF (UK) Ltd
150 Wharfedale Road
Winnersh Triangle
Wokingham
Berkshire  RG41 5RB
United Kingdom
Tel: +44(0)118 918 6500
Fax: +44(0)118 969 9749
E-mail: service@itsmf.co.uk
www.itsmf.co.uk

OGC
Rosebery Court
St Andrews Business Park
Norwich  NR7 0HS
United Kingdom
Tel: +44(0)1603 704567
Fax: +44(0)1603 704817
E-mail: info@ogc.gov.uk
www.ogc.gov.uk
www.itil.co.uk

British Standards Institution
389 Chiswick High Road
London  W4 4AL
United Kingdom
Tel: +44(0)208 996 9001
Fax: +44(0)208 996 7001
E-mail: info@bsi-global.com
www.bsi-global.com

APM Group Limited
Sword House
Totteridge Road
High Wycombe
Buckinghamshire HP13 6DG
United Kingdom
Tel: +44 (0) 1494 452 450
Fax: +44 (0) 1494 459 559
E-mail: servicedesk@apmgroup.co.uk
www.apmgroup.co.uk

TSO
PO Box 29
Norwich NR3 1GN
United Kingdom
Tel: +44(0) 870 600 5522
Fax: +44(0) 870 600 5533
E-mail: customer.services@tso.co.uk
www.tso.co.uk

# Best Practice with ITIL

The ITIL V3 publication portfolio consists of a unique library of titles that offer guidance on quality IT services and best practices. Used by hundreds of the world's most successful organizations, its five core titles are available in a range of formats.

Manual/hard copy (M)
PDF e-book (P)
On-line subscription (O)

| | |
|---|---|
| ITIL Lifecycle Suite<br>(All five books) | M ISBN: 9780113310616<br>P ISBN: 9780113310623<br>O ISBN: 7003171 |
| Service Strategy | M ISBN: 9780113310456<br>P ISBN: 9780113310524<br>O ISBN: 7003147 |
| Service Design | M ISBN: 9780113310470<br>P ISBN: 9780113310548<br>O ISBN: 7003148 |
| Service Transition | M ISBN: 9780113310487<br>P ISBN: 9780113310555<br>O ISBN: 7003155 |
| Service Operation | M ISBN: 9780113310463<br>P ISBN: 9780113310531<br>O ISBN: 7003156 |
| Continual Service Improvement | M ISBN: 9780113319494<br>P ISBN: 9780113310562<br>O ISBN: 7003157 |
| Official Introduction to the<br>ITIL Service Lifecycle | M ISBN: 9780113310616<br>P ISBN: 9780113310623<br>O ISBN: 7003171 |

# About itSMF

The itSMF is the only truly independent and internationally recognized forum for IT Service Management professionals worldwide. This not-for-profit organization is a prominent player in the on-going development and promotion of IT Service Management "best practice", standards and qualifications and has been since 1991.

Globally, the itSMF now boasts over 6000 member companies, blue chip and public sector alike, covering in excess of 70,000 individuals spread over 40+ international Chapters.

Each chapter is a separate legal entity and is largely autonomous. The UK Chapter has over 16,000 members: it offers a flourishing annual conference, online bookstore, regular regional meetings and special interest groups and numerous other benefits for members. Its website is at www.itsmf.co.uk.

There is a separate International entity that provides an overall steering and support function to existing and emerging chapters. It has its own website at www.itsmf.org.

# Best Management Practice Partnership

### UK Government and Best Practice
The Office of Government Commerce (OGC), as an office of HM Treasury, plays a vital role in developing methodologies, processes and frameworks and establishing these as Best Practice.

The huge growth in the market for OGC's Best Practice guidance is evidence of how highly it is valued - proving that it offers not just theory but workable business solutions. ITIL® is now the most widely accepted approach to service management in the world, while PRINCE2™ has established itself as a global leader in project management.

OGC, on behalf of the UK government, remains committed to maintaining and developing the guidance. Through an innovative and successful partnering arrangement, OGC is able to ensure that users are supported by high quality publications, training, qualification schemes and consultancy services.

### OGC and its official partners
In 2006, OGC completed an open competitive procurement and appointed The Stationery Office (TSO) as official publisher and the APM Group Ltd (APMG) as official accreditor. Together they have created the Best Management Practice, as the official home of OGC's Best Practice guidance. The partners are committed to delivering, supporting and endorsing the very best products and services in the marketplace.

### The Stationery Office (TSO)
TSO draws upon over 200 years of print and publishing services experience, and is the only official publisher for OGC's Best Practice guidance.
TSO also manages the various refresh projects on OGC's behalf and ensures that the quality of the guidance is maintained at the highest possible level. A dedicated team serves the Best Management Practice community, providing newsletters, updates and latest information on the products and current projects.

## *APM Group (APMG)*

APMG is a global business providing accreditation and certification services. It is one of the first medium-sized companies to establish an independent Ethics and Standards Board to monitor its business practice and to help ensure it supports the industries it serves in a transparent and responsible way.

APMG has been instrumental in helping to establish PRINCE2™ as an international standard and now provides global accreditation schemes in ITIL®, PRINCE2™, MSP™ (Managing Successful Programmes) and M_o_R® (Management Of Risk).

## *Keep up to date with Best Management Practice*

The Best Management Practice Knowledge Centre brings together the official partners and recognized user groups to create a comprehensive source of information. Here you can find articles, white papers, book reviews and events, as well as links to the individual product sites.

Visit www.best-management-practice.com.